MW01247543

SONYA H. FLOYD

WESTBOW
PRESS*
A DIVISION OF THOMAS NELSON
& ZONDERVAN

WestBow Press books may be ordered through booksellers or by contacting:

WestBow Press
A Division of Thomas Nelson & Zondervan
1663 Liberty Drive
Bloomington, IN 47403
www.westbowpress.com
844-714-3454

Scripture taken from the King James Version of the Bible.

ISBN: 979-8-3850-2479-7 (sc)
ISBN: 979-8-3850-2480-3 (hc)
ISBN: 979-8-3850-2481-0 (e)

Library of Congress Control Number: 2024908826

Print information available on the last page.

WestBow Press rev. date: 05/14/2024

Contents

My Best Friend

SO MUCH HAS HAPPENED in my life. As I look back on it now, it seems impossible that I could have made so many mistakes in such a short period. I married in 1966 while I was still in high school. I gave birth to my baby girl in September 1968 after graduating in June, divorced my first husband in 1969, and remarried my second husband in 1970. Wow! What went wrong? Everything! Here is how it went down—the good, the bad, and the ugly.

Although I was saved during a Billy Graham crusade in Charlotte, North Carolina, at the age of thirteen, I became bitter toward God when my parents divorced when I was fourteen years old. Therefore, not being mature in Christ or even involved in any church anywhere, against my mother's wishes, I married my high school sweetheart. The only problem was that I was not out of high school. We were married two weeks before my eleventh-grade year ended and after he had graduated.

We were married without my parents' blessing. It was not legal then to be married in North Carolina before the age of eighteen, so we eloped and went to South Carolina. Also, we were not allowed to attend high school while married, which created a problem for me in my senior year. I managed to keep it a secret from school staff, although a few of my friends knew we had gotten married. My husband had already graduated and would attend college in the fall. I worked after school with one of my favorite teachers, who actually paid me to help her grade papers from the Spanish classes she taught at our school. I also worked at a local grocery store every day after school until eight thirty or nine at night.

I worked hard to maintain my grades, keep our small two-bedroom mobile home clean, and work after school. Nothing seemed to overwhelm me until I started throwing up during first-period class in January after being married for only eight months. I had no idea what was wrong and was totally in shock when my doctor told me I was pregnant. I was almost six months into my senior year. But I had four and a half months to go. What in this world was I going to do?

I immediately talked to my first-period teacher, the same one I worked for after school. She agreed that I should not let the other staff know of my situation; otherwise, I may have to drop out of school. She allowed me to miss first-period Spanish class and make it up at the end of the day. She knew I was married and had kept it from everyone, but she was upset that I had messed up my college plans. She helped me so much and encouraged me.

When my condition became evident, I had a quick solution. Everyone over fifty years of age will remember the "tent dress." We were not allowed to wear pants in school, only dresses, and thank goodness the tent dress was very popular. It covered a multitude of pounds and lost waistlines. My sister made several of these wonderful dresses for me, and all my friends were wearing the same style, so no one was the wiser about my predicament.

Everything seemed fine. I had gotten over my morning sickness, and I continued working after school. I graduated in June. My husband worked with my brother-in-law at a local grocery store and attended classes at the local college during the day. To the outside world, all was well. But on the inside, I was falling apart.

Once I became pregnant, everything changed. My husband told me right away that a baby was not what we needed right now in our marriage with both of us still in school. *Hello!* I thought. *I did not do this alone. How do you not need a baby already growing inside my body?*

As a young girl, I had dreamed of marriage and children—lots and lots of children—but now all my dreams were dashed as this man I married told me that he did not want children. He began staying at work late—very late. On many occasions, he did not come home at all. By the time the baby came, he was nowhere to be seen. As a matter of fact, I was alone at the hospital. My sister came to be with me, but he never came.

After a very hard labor, I delivered a beautiful baby girl. I was feeling so depressed. My thoughts were all negative. *Why had I not listened to Mama or God? What had I done? How was I going to take care of a baby alone?* He obviously was not returning, and although I was with my sister and my mother who were taking care of me, I would have to be on my own. I knew it. I was depressed, alone, and so very afraid. Deep depression came over me, and I spent many nights crying and blaming my husband, God, and everyone except myself.

While I sat in the mire of my depression, the thought, which only God had put deep into my soul, suddenly came to me that God knew. He had not been sitting in heaven one day and said, "Hey, angels, I did not see this coming. I did not know Sonya would go through all this, get married, have a baby, and be unhappy. What has happened to Sonya?"

He knew. He knew all along what was going to happen. He knew I would not listen to my mother. He knew I would sin. He knew I would be depressed. As I sat there crying, feeling sorry for myself, and holding this beautiful baby girl, God spoke to me in a way I could understand. Suddenly, I realized He was not mad at me for my rebellion or marriage. During all this confusion, He had sent me a gift, a beautiful gift that needed me, one I needed with all my heart, someone I could hold on to, a true blessing straight from Him. Although I had left God, He had never left me. She was not an accident but a blessing from almighty God, my miracle. She would help me return to Him, to return to His way and not my way. The two of us would become the best of friends. We had our whole life ahead of us, and with God, all things are possible. And what He had in store for us was remarkable.

By the way, she's now fifty-five, and I'm seventy-four. We're still best friends!

The Miracle Son

WHEN MY SECOND HUSBAND, Dan, and I got married, we both knew that we wanted children, lots and lots of children. We both came from large families, and we both had three sisters and two brothers. We had a beautiful daughter. (Remember, she's my best friend.) Thus began one of the hardest journeys we had to travel. Going into this journey, I knew it would not be easy. I'd had a very hard time delivering my daughter. The on-call doctor who delivered her said that having children should never be my goal in life, using those exact words.

My life was more beautiful during this time than it had ever been. We had our first little house out in the country and a beautiful, healthy daughter. We both had good jobs. It seemed like this was the perfect time to try for this family addition. We had no earthly idea what God had in store for the two of us who wanted children so badly.

I began seeking a good gynecologist in our area and received several referrals from friends and family. Test after test and doctor after doctor (five actually) revealed that it would be literally impossible for me to have another baby. But I refused to give up. After all, look at what God had done for me already. He was—and is—my God of the second chance, and I knew He was a miracle-working God. Even though the doctors had said it was impossible, I knew all things were possible with God. So I adopted some real prayer warriors, mainly Dan's mother, and started praying.

After two long years, it finally happened. When Dan and I went to our doctor, the last one who had performed all the tests and showed us how impossible it would be, my happiness turned to distress when he told us that getting pregnant would not mean that I would carry this child to full term. But I did!

It was not easy. Dan's mother came over many days to babysit Shelly while I lay so still, not daring to lift my head. When I did, everything would fall apart. Keeping food inside became my lifelong goal. After ten or twelve weeks of this sickness, I carried my little one fine for the remainder of my pregnancy. I even returned to work for our family doctor.

After seventy-two hours of labor and several weeks in the hospital after his birth, we took home our beautiful baby boy. He was the apple of his sister's eye. She immediately became his second little mother. All of this had become such a miracle. However, God had only begun. This child would be the beginning of another miracle, one that changed my husband's life forever.

When Matt was eight weeks young, he developed pneumonia. It was the beginning of fall, and we had the worst rainfall we had ever seen. It had rained nonstop for three full days and nights. Our fields and yard were flooded, and getting to the car was almost like swimming a marathon. It was Friday night, and I called Dr. Singletary, my boss, and asked him to meet us at the hospital. Since he could hear Matt wheezing over the phone, he suggested he should come to our house because of the torrential rain.

Not only did he come, but he put an oxygen tent over our son's crib, slept on our couch, and stayed with us from Friday night through Sunday until the danger was over and the rain had stopped. Dr. Singletary has been gone many years now, but I often think of what might have happened had God not sent him that night to save our son.

After he left, I saw my husband, who was not a Christian at this time, on his knees in front of our son's crib, thanking God for saving him and promising God that he would be in church on Sunday if God would just let him live. God did, and we did. Several weeks later, Dan gave his life to Christ, which opened up a life of miracles that only God could perform!

Not Without My Sister

THE DEPARTMENT OF SOCIAL Services had asked us if they could place teenagers in our home just on the weekend to try to find places of permanent residence for them. Some of these teens were actually having problems in their foster homes. Since I almost had a nervous breakdown when we had to return a baby, we had decided that small babies that DSS could move were not our calling. So we decided we could help with teenagers. After all, who wanted to permanently keep teenagers? We would just help them through their situation and allow them to return to their foster homes. Yeah right!

Patricia was an absolute beauty. She was our first weekender. She had a delicately small frame and beautiful golden hair that landed right at her tiny waistline. Hers had been a horrible nightmare of a childhood. She came from a dysfunctional family filled with violence and abuse. Her mother was imprisoned for stabbing her father, and Patricia and her sisters were sent to live with a grandmother who absolutely despised them. Living with a grandparent who does not want you was better than the life they had before this grandparent.

While living with their mother, she invited a man, Tommy, to live with them, and he immediately began molesting the girls in the family. Two of the girls had children by this man. As soon as Patricia was nine years old, Tommy told her she would be next and she was to be ready for him when he came into her room.

Patricia barred the door with the only piece of furniture in the room, an old chest. Then she took her seven-year-old sister, Brenda, and they ran for their life. Unfortunately, a police officer picked up both girls and returned them home, where Tommy promptly took a tobacco stick and beat Patricia, breaking her arm. He told her if she told anyone about the incident, he would kill her the next time.

The next day at school, Patricia didn't say a word. Her arm was swollen, and she could not write. But when the teacher asked what happened, she told them she had fallen. When the teachers asked Brenda what happened, she told them the whole story of how he had beaten her sister. Both girls were removed from the home.

When Patricia first came to our home, we fell totally in love with her. She was so helpful with the smaller children, our own son and daughter. She loved both of them very much. And they adored her.

One night after all the children were in bed, I passed by Patricia's room and heard her crying. I slipped quietly into her room and found her weeping. When I asked if I could help, she told me she missed her sister and she knew Brenda was not happy in a foster home without her. We soon made arrangements for

Brenda to live with her sister, and both girls became a wonderful part of our lives.

These girls came to Christ with open arms. Both girls were so full of gratitude for being out of their situation and into a stable home. There was no bitterness and no hatred of their parents. They were just thankful to Jesus and very appreciative to now have a heavenly Father who loved them and cared for them in ways they had never known before.

Both of these girls continued to visit their family members. They helped them monetarily, took food, and loved their mom until the day she died. They never condemned her but prayed for her on a regular basis. They also witnessed to their sisters and all their family members, trying to bring them to Christ.

Both girls are happily married now and have children and grandchildren. We did not have a lot of money when they came to live with us, but we did have a loving Savior who said, "I will supply all your needs." And He did. Only God!

Please, Daddy, Don't Leave Me Here

LIFE WITH TEENAGERS, ESPECIALLY troubled or traumatized teens, was not always pleasant, but one of the hardest and saddest decisions we ever had to make in our home was returning one of our girls, who had been with us a while, to her elderly grandmother. After being warned three different times that sneaking out of the house at night would not be tolerated, she decided she could continue to disobey. We had discussed the fact that anything could happen to a fourteen-year-old when she was out at night. The other girls living in our home were becoming uneasy with her behavior, and although they loved her very much, they would let us know when she did the vanishing act out of the bedroom window.

Fearing our other girls might follow suit and after much prayer, Dan sat her down. This was the conversation.

"Young lady, you have been warned over and over again about sneaking out of the house at night, and it seems you really want your freedom and to do things your way. When you came to live with us, we offered you a home, a life, and a future, and the only thing we ask is that you obey some very simple rules. One of these rules is that you never go out at night alone—ever. Anything could happen to you. Yet you have continued to disobey and sneak out at night. What can we do to remedy that? We cannot and will not allow it."

I will never forget the look on this precious teenager's face. With a very stoic and defiant look, she proclaimed, "Just take me to my grandmother's house. I can live with her."

The only problem was that Grandmother was too old and feeble to care for such a young and troubled teenager.

Hers had been a life of disappointment. Cheryl's father had died in a car wreck on his way to work when she was two years of age. Her mom tried to take care of the five children left behind but soon turned to prescription drugs and then later added alcohol. Knowing she couldn't cope, family members forced her to call DSS to take the children. When she was only three years old, Cheryl and her brothers were placed in an orphanage. At this orphanage, she wrote her mom many letters, begging her to come and get her. Mom never came. She died when Cheryl was thirteen years old. How well I remember talking Cheryl into burying that box of letters, the ones begging her mom to come get her, in our backyard so she could put that sad part of her little life behind her.

She came to our home as a precious but broken young teenager. She was looking for love and found the love of Jesus one night after attending a church service. We always had devotions at night, and all the kids would hop on our king-sized bed to end our day with prayer. We had the wonderful opportunity of leading her to Christ and knew she understood what He had done for her. I know, beyond any doubt, that Christ came into her life that night. It was what I clung to after she left our home and was out on her own in a world where Satan is alive and well and seeking to devour our young teenagers.

Dan asked again, "Are you sure you want to leave here and live with your grandmother or go back to DSS because I will not allow your disobedience any longer?"

Here, a child, making an adult choice, wanted to be free at last, running, forever running. This took our Cheryl away from us.

We packed her small suitcase of earthly belongings, and Dan took her to her grandmother's house, which was very small, dark, and dingy. I remember crying and asking Dan to give her another chance, and he said she had three already and she had to want to stay. She had to want to do what was right. God had to allow her to travel her path, to learn to trust in Him and Him alone.

Her life took many sad turns. Happily married but not finding what she was looking for, she ran again. Pregnancy and having a daughter did not bring happiness. Divorce did not bring happiness. Remarriage did not bring happiness. She was always running. We did not see Cheryl for many years, and when we did see her, she was working hard, a mother with a beautiful daughter. She was now remarried, attending church and serving the Lord in her community and her home. At our home, Cheryl had opened her heart to the Lord, though it took a painful journey for her to find He is trustworthy.

Christians aren't perfect. Being saved by grace does not mean that she didn't have to suffer consequences. God had been drawing her to Him from the time she left that orphanage because she was desperately looking for a father. He allowed us to fill in the gap. But He promised He would take away that lonely, longing heart and in its place put a heart that could follow Him. We lovingly took her back, assured her that we had missed her, and prayed for her, and she and her family again became part of the Floyd family! God's Word says that if we stay faithful, He will restore to us even the years that the locust has eaten (Joel 2:25). Cheryl wrote Dan this on Father's Day in 2018.

Happy Father's Day to my earthly dad. He taught me so much and helped mold me into the person I am today. I was lost when I met him and saved now because he showed me the way to Jesus. Not many orphans or foster children get the opportunity to have awesome parents like God blessed me with at such a difficult time in my life's journey. Thank you, Dad. I wish you a wonderful Father's Day, and I thank you daily for being the dad you didn't have to be. I thank you for sharing true family love with me. I thank you for leading me to a life with Jesus. I thank you for accepting me back in after I left. My story with you is like the parable in the Bible, the prodigal son. That was me. I thought there was so much more life out there that I had to keep running to find. I lost my way, going through the worst times of my life. I realized the errors of my ways. Your arms welcomed me back and never judged. Thank you for that. There is no man on the face of this earth that I respect more than you. Today, I want to publicly thank you for accepting me, loving me like I am your own, and allowing me back into the family after I lost my way. I love you. Happy Father's Day.

Years later, I was talking to the girls about things they might have changed in their lives, and Cheryl emphatically said, "I would have chased his car as he drove away that night, leaving me standing there, and I would have begged him, 'Please, Daddy, don't leave me here.' My life would have been different. I stayed up all night that horrible night, watching roaches climb the wall and knowing mice were on the floor, but my proud heart would not allow me to go back to the safe haven I left behind."

But God had other plans for Cheryl, ones to teach her to rely on a heavenly Father instead of an earthly one. "For I know the plans I have for you, declares the Lord, and you shall seek Me, and find Me when you search for me with all your heart" (Jeremiah 29:11–13).

The Coat

MY FIRST REACTION WAS, "Absolutely not. We do not have room. Where are we going to put her?"

The car was full with the eight of us, including all our luggage and food for the weekend. We had been offered a weekend at a beautiful house in Brevard, North Carolina, that belonged to my husband's boss, all for free with no strings attached. It was just us and all our kids in a well-packed station wagon I had been packing all day while the kids were at school and Dan was finishing his last bit of work on a beautiful Friday afternoon in early September. I had spent all morning making sandwiches and brownies so we could picnic on the way and not have to stop at a fast-food joint on the way, which we could not afford!

Twylia came home from school very upset. One of her best friends from school was in the emergency room at our local hospital. Her father had beaten her, and she had a few broken ribs. Twylia began immediately to ask if we would get her, saying she just could not leave her there in the emergency room alone.

My question was, "Where are we going to put her?" We were ready to leave and drive out of the driveway the minute Dan got home from work.

Twylia responded, "I will let her sit on my lap all the way to wherever we are going if you will just go see about her."

As I made my last trip into the house, the phone rang. DSS was asking if I could possibly take one more teenager just for the weekend until they could find a place for her to stay. (We all know how that turned out!)

As soon as Dan got home, we did not go to the mountains. Instead we went to the emergency room and picked up Debby, whose ribs were bound with tape and who sat squished between Brenda and Twylia all the way to our friend's mountain house.

Yes, Debby did come to stay with us. After that weekend, we all were in love with her and she with us. We honestly hoped DSS could not find another home for her, and all the girls had already agreed on where she would sleep and with whom. (We had two to each bed.) They also agreed to share their clothes with Debby because she left with nothing and she had to have clothes for school. Everyone shared, so Debby stayed and started school with our other girls.

One afternoon, I got a call from Bonnie Stuckey, the wife of Dan's boss.

She said, "Sonya, I would not want to offend in any way, but I have three big boxes of clothes. I know that you and Dan have taken in those teenagers, and I wanted to know if you would like to have them."

Well, I was not offended in any way and very thankful that she called me. Her clothes were beautiful, and she would often fly to New York to shop. I was very excited. Dan brought home three large boxes of beautiful clothes that night.

The girls were ecstatic! They started to try on clothes, and as only God can provide, they fit as if they were made for them. We were hoping there was a coat for Debby. She did not have a coat for school. As each girl continued to find clothes that fit, they modeled and walked around the den area in each new outfit.

At the very bottom of the last box was a beautiful coat. Again, the fit was perfect for Debby. She tried it on and claimed it, and everyone was happy.

However, three minutes after the den was cleaned, after the boxes had been thrown away and all the clothing had been claimed and taken to be hung in their closets, Debby came running back to the den, holding the coat in her hands with tears streaming down her cheeks.

"Look at the inside tag. Look at what it says!" There, beautifully printed on a designer tag—the Designer being God Himself—was "A Debby Roberts original—from Massey's of New York."

Could we really think that it would be a coincidence that Debby, who had just received Christ as her Savior one week prior to this, was named Debby Roberts? Not only did He supply her the one item she needed for school, but He also put her name on it. He is such an awesome God who says, "And my God shall supply all your need according to His riches in glory by Christ Jesus" (Philippians 4:19).

Will You Take My Baby?

HAVING FIVE TEENAGERS AT home, one preteen, and one eight-year-old son, my days became busy and long. The girls who had come to live with us had substandard grades. Dan and I had decided as soon as we got them that their academic achievements were tantamount to their spiritual growth. We had to find a way to help these girls secure their future.

We restricted television during the weeknights. We worked hard on grades and made sure that each child had homework done right after dinner and before bed. The exception was Monday night when we all gathered around our console television, sitting on the couch and floor and enjoying the largest bag of Doritos and M&Ms our grocer could provide. Believe me when I say it was really a treat and they didn't last long between seven children and Charlie and his mom, Kathy, who was living with us at the time and another miracle entirely.

During all this hustle and bustle of living, working, and raising seven kids, I became overwhelmed. Driving to and from

Florence to work and taking kids to school was taking its toll on my physical being. After much prayer and trust in God, Dan decided it was time for me to take a break from work and concentrate on raising five teenage girls, a son and daughter of our own, and Kathy and Charlie. *A break from work?* I thought. *What was he thinking?*

Until this break, I had been a paralegal in a law firm for many years. God had allowed me to become a part of a firm that felt like family, and they wished me luck and cheered me on as I decided to leave the firm. Little did they know that God would use them in a great way later in our lives.

I was sitting in my rocking chair, quilting a blanket for our youngest daughter, when I heard a car drive up in our driveway. From that small white car came a petite woman holding a heavy baby boy. It was extremely cold that day, and I noticed he only had on a small T-shirt and a diaper that looked to weigh about five pounds. He was absolutely beautiful with a head full of blonde hair and the saddest eyes I had ever seen.

Opening the door, I asked the young lady if I could help her. I thought maybe she was lost and looking for someone. She quickly asked me if I kept children. Not understanding her question, I asked if she were looking for a nursery for her son.

She replied, "No, I heard that you kept children."

I tried to explain that I had recently acquired five teenagers but that I did not *keep* children. She then looked toward the car in the driveway, handed me her son, and said, "Will you take my baby?"

She then turned and ran to get in the car with a man and drove out of our driveway. I stood stunned, holding one of the most beautiful children I had ever seen, with no clothes, no diapers, nothing. But worst of all, no name! She had left me her son and not told me his name.

I stood there for a moment and then quickly took him to the rocking chair, where I tried to cuddle him and warm him by the fire. He stared into my face with a stoic expression of nothingness, no smile, no tears, no joy, just nothingness. I called my husband, who left his job a few blocks from home and brought me diapers and some baby T-shirts from a local store. We spent his lunch hour playing and holding this beautiful baby boy.

When our girls came home from school, they too fell in love with our new addition. After several days, one of our daughters said a friend, the aunt of our little one, approached her, saying he belonged to her sister, who was on drugs and living with a man who did not like children. The baby's name was Michael. Praise the Lord! We had another small rooster in the midst of our hens, and he had a name, Michael!

We loved Michael from the very beginning. He was the best baby. He never, ever cried. Even when he hurt himself, he never cried. We found out that he was almost six months old. After his first doctor's visit, we discovered he didn't cry because he had been fed Valium, crushed and put into his bottles of milk while he was left alone in a mobile home in a crib while adults went to parties for drugs and alcohol, leaving this precious baby alone to fend for himself.

As cruel as it was, God never abandoned this baby. Michael learned at six months of age how to escape from a crib. We discovered this when he would show up beside my bed every morning, holding onto our comforter as he pulled his little body up to the side of the bed and gazed into my eyes. We planted a camera inside the closet of his little room and watched as he stood in his crib, throwing his little chubby foot up and over the top of the crib until it finally caught his big toe. Then he lifted his body over the side, dropping down to the floor and shaking himself like a little puppy, never crying. Then he crawled around the den and into my bedroom, where he stood quietly beside my bed until I opened my eyes. Our very own little Houdini!

Like I said, Michael never cried. His addiction to Valium and his ability to accept pain, like when he hit the floor, was amazing but saddening at the same time. It was a blessed and happy day when all of our family got to see Michael cry.

It happened like this. We were all sitting at the table eating, and I had bought baby food in jars for Michael. He had never had baby food, only Valium-laced milk in bottles. I opened the first jar and began to spoon it into his little mouth. He loved it. He wanted more and more. After two full jars of food, he began reaching for the empty jar.

My husband said, "Give him another one."

I said, "If I give him another jar, he is going to be sick."

Dan said, "Give it to him anyway. He acts like he is starving."

I opened another jar and then another until finally, after four jars of food, he did get sick. And when he got sick, he started to cry, and so did we. We all sat around that table, holding him and crying. I really believe this was the first time in his little life that he had ever felt safe and secure, and at that moment in time, he knew he was home.

Michael slept with us in our bed for a few weeks because I was worried that he would continue to get out of his crib and fall onto the floor and hurt himself. After his bloodwork came back clean, he began to act like a normal baby. He soon realized that if he just stood up in his crib, shook that railing, or made some noise, someone would soon come to his rescue.

We eventually adopted Michael. Remember the law firm I mentioned before? Jack Lawson, who is now in heaven with our Savior, did the adoption free of charge. His mother gave him to us after we offered her a home and security from her drug lord. My husband gave up his little office space to make a room for her and Michael. The only stipulation was that she had to go back to school. She could have lived free and raised her son, and I would have kept him while she attended school.

We really thought it would work, but after eight days, she left in the middle of the night and left a note saying she had to have her drugs and we could have Michael. My heart broke for her, but at the same time, my heart rejoiced at the opportunity to have another son. Our son, Matt, was the only boy in a home full of girls. He was especially happy and loved Michael from the very beginning. They became best friends, and Matt did everything with him.

Michael is forty-two now. He has a remembrance of his childhood. His big toe is deformed slightly because of all the Houdini tricks he accomplished before he could even walk. The Bible says in Isaiah 51:1 for us to remember the pit we escaped from and where we could have been. He was not saved then, but he is saved now. As sad as his beginning was, it was good for him. It made him stronger for some terrible trials he would face in his future. He's been through tougher times than his first six months, but he was stronger because of his first six months. God made him strong to face life from the very beginning. Believe me, if any of us were ever stranded on an island, we would want Michael. He would find a way. He would keep us safe, and he would bring us home. Psalm 127:3 says, "Behold, children are a heritage from the Lord," no matter how they came to us. Thank You, God, for sending us the miracle of Michael.

I Want Your Bed

SITTING IN OUR DEN at one thirty in the morning, I plainly heard the words spoken as if someone were standing directly behind me. Since the only two in the room were myself and Lady, our dog of six years, I was certain that my husband had entered the room. I turned to see why he would say to me, "I want your bed."

He was in our bed. Why would he want my bed, and why did I not hear him come down the hall and into the dining area where I sat writing in the early morning hours? As I turned to greet him, I realized no one was there. It was just us two, Lady and I, still and quiet in the early morning hours.

Continuing my Bible study, I heard it again, much more clearly and with full understanding that I was completely alone, for I had walked down the hall the first time to see if Dan were in fact still in our bed. And he was sound asleep.

Yes, I had heard it this time, loud and clear, in the very depth of my spirit. My problem was that I did not believe what I was hearing. To describe my feeling at this very moment, I must explain what had happened to lead to this moment in my life.

Life was beautiful. For the very first time in our lives, we believed that God was in control of everything. We finally reached a point in our lives where we believed we were completely in God's will. The previous years of struggle had finally ended when we had successfully sold our business and found ourselves with money not earmarked for bills, children, medical issues, or anything. Just money!

Wow, what a blessing to have money to do with as we pleased. But our heart was to please God, to do with our money whatever His will was in our lives. There were eight children, remember? We would give them money to pay off all their houses and give them cars, things we could never afford while they were home. Now, we could help them. Or could we?

The more we thought about these things, the more God impressed upon our hearts that giving to these eight children was not such a good idea. First and foremost, the children were all doing fine. Each had their own lives, their own children, and their own security, and at that time, each were in church and serving God in some way or another. Yes, there were struggles. One couple was struggling to stay together. One couple was having trouble with a child using drugs. One couple was facing cancer within her own family, but all were facing life. And God was providing. He did not need help from us.

As we prayed and consulted a wonderful team of experts, as God's Word says to seek counsel when making life-changing decisions, at PNC Bank, we heard stories of other families whose names were never disclosed but had given all their wealth to children and grandchildren, much to their demise. Was this a wise thing? Did we want to give money to children to enable them to get a divorce or support a drug habit? No, of course not. We wanted God's will for our lives and theirs too.

So with our children's blessings, we consulted an estate planning group from our friends at PNC who helped us plan our future, a future described in Jeremiah 29:13, "and ye shall seek me, and find me, when ye shall search for me with all your heart."

During this seeking and searching for God's will in our lives, God impressed upon my heart to start Shepherds Rest, a place of rest for God's servants. These men and women were giving their lives in full-time service to our Lord. Our church was becoming one of the fastest-growing churches in our state, with fourteen active campuses and nearly three hundred employees. Some of these young couples had several children and not a lot of money. We could use the homes God had given us to open our doors and allow them to come and have a peaceful and quiet time at no cost to them. It would be a resort of sorts for pastors and their wives, to reconnect and have a romantic weekend away from work, children, business, and so forth, to have time to reconnect with God and reflect on what is important in their lives. Thus, Shepherds Rest was born, a retreat for pastors and wives for NewSpring Church—and little did we know—many other churches as well.

We made a brochure with colored pictures of our homes on a lake and the home we had purchased right after selling the business in the North Carolina mountains. Since our youth, it was a dream we had always had to own a house in the mountains.

Now, back to my bed! Why would God be telling me that He wanted my bed? Had I not just described to you that we had given Him everything? We had opened our home in South Carolina located on a beautiful lake, and my husband would fill up the pontoon boat and jet ski and make arrangements to cook his delicious fish or steak while people were visiting. Or we would take them out to dinner. We'd do anything to make them feel special and have an awesome weekend. That was our goal. Our house has two beautiful guest rooms where flowers would be placed by the bed and coffee would fill the air every morning, thanks to our beautiful daughter, Shelly, who cleans and puts fresh flowers in the rooms and makes sure everything is perfect. A theater room in the basement is there for their entertainment, and people could slide off the sliding board right down into the water at the end of the pier. Our bedroom is located on the middle floor below the two beautiful guest rooms. Our bedroom is special. For fifty-three years, that is exactly what it has been, our bedroom. It's special, just ours.

The only thing we really wanted after we sold the company was a house in the mountains. Our beautiful mountain house has several guest rooms, a theater room, and a beautiful view. Again, our bedroom is on the middle floor and is special. It's ours. For fifty years, it has been just ours.

Do you see what God is asking? It is the only thing we have left. We've given Him every house: every room, every boat, every car, everything. You can come and play, eat, and enjoy the baby grand piano, but the only thing you cannot do is sleep in my bed, my special place. It was ours for fifty years already! And why would God want my bed when the guest room beds were just as beautiful? I guess I'll find the answer to that question when I see Him face-to-face. God was the only one who knew how I felt about our bed. He was the only one who knew I did not like guests in my bed. After all, that is what guest rooms were for, right?

But I know one thing for sure. The moment I said, "Yes, Lord, you can have my bed," I felt an overwhelming peace, a completeness I had never felt. Since then, we have received dozens of letters from couples who said they had never experienced such rest and recuperation at any place they had every slept previously. It's been amazing. Most couples who come now sleep in our bed, in our room, our secret place that only God knew I didn't want to give up. That was exactly what He wanted, anything I didn't want to give up. He wants it all. And when we give it all to Him, He can do so much with it. He blesses it, expands it, makes it beautiful to many, and fills it with peace that passes all understanding. A very wise woman, Lori, told me one time that every little thing you own owns a little piece of you. I can honestly tell you that since I gave God my bed, I have never been more at peace. Sometimes we give God our children; then we take them back. Sometimes we give God our finances; then we take them back. I'm trying to give God everything. He does so much more with it than I could ever imagine. He does so much for me that I could never, ever repay, sending His only Son to die for me. Wow, how could I not give Him my bed?

Miracle: Courtesy of Curtis Mathis

REMEMBERING MIRACLES IN OUR lives makes this next one a classic. The title of this book, *Only God*, brings this to light. My husband, Dan, had only been saved a few months. Church became an awesome part of our lives. We loved hearing God's Word and growing in it every day. One Sunday, our pastor preached a sermon on tithing that lit a fire in us that has burned brightly our entire fifty-four years of marriage.

Dan and I both had fathers who drank a lot and mothers who prayed a lot. As young adults and before marriage, these praying mothers taught us that tithing was of God and a good thing. Since Dan was a new believer, we decided that from that sermon forward, we would start tithing. Sounds simple, right? It was anything but simple!

It was not simple because during this time in our early marriage, we did not have enough money at the end of our week to have lunch money. We had our very first 1,200-square-foot new home. This very small home came with a payment book.

We had a five-year-old daughter and a newborn son, whom the doctors said I could never have.

Since I had not yet returned to work after his birth, things were tight, very tight. I can remember when I worked at a law office in our town, the girls would ask me to lunch, and I would always tell them I was busy or I had to run home and do something, but the truth was that I did not have money for lunch. Often, Dan and I both would have a pack of cheese crackers and a Coke for lunch. Like I said, it was tight, very tight.

During this first week of this new venture in obeying God, I sat down and added up all our bills to see if it would be possible for us to pay everything and still pay our tithes. I added it over and over. No way. It was impossible.

When Dan came home from work that evening, I told him the bad news. We discussed that it would be impossible to start tithing right then. Our bills took all our money every week. We also discussed that in his sermon, our pastor had said, "Don't pray about it. Just do it." In order to do it, some priorities had to be rearranged.

About two months before this sermon, we had purchased a console, a Curtis Mathis color television. We had borrowed the money from a small finance company in our small town of Lake City, South Carolina. Our payments were $28 per month. It sounds like a small-enough payment, but to us at that time in our lives, it was a big deal. Since this was the smallest of our payments, we decided we would use this money to pay our tithes. We went to the manager of the finance company and told him we would not be able to make our payment this month. He knew us personally because we had used this company to buy all the furniture in our home. We told him we would make two payments next month, and he told us that would be fine.

We were so excited. We had stepped out on faith and decided to take God at His Word and start tithing. This was always the first check we wrote, and as we began the journey with God, an incredible thing happened. It became easier! I started back to work after four months, which made it easier to make all our payments and continue to tithe.

One afternoon, I came home from work during lunch and found a check in our mailbox from the IRS. I immediately called Dan and asked why we should receive a check from the government when tax time and refund checks (state and federal) had already come in and been spent six months ago. At any rate, it was made out to us in the sum of $349.27. We were ecstatic. Since the Curtis Mathis television we were enjoying was the only payment from a finance company, with high interest rates, we decided to go there and pay this check on the balance of our television.

The next day after work and before closing time, I went to the finance company and asked for the balance of our bill. When he brought me the bill, I stared at it in total shock. Quickly, I looked for the deposit slip where I had just deposited the IRS check we had received. There it was, $349.27!

When Dan came home that night, we really rejoiced together. God showed us early in our marriage that if we wanted Him to take care of us, we must trust and obey Him, even if it does not add up, even if there is not enough, even when doctors tell us there is no way! He is our way. He is enough, and He will provide.

$349.27 was not a coincidence. It was sent to us by an almighty God who said, "Bring ye all the tithes into the storehouse, and prove me, if I will not open you the windows of heaven, and pour out a blessing that there shall not be room enough to receive it" (Malachi 3:10).

The Devine Appointment

ONE SATURDAY AFTERNOON, I found myself in downtown Florence, visiting all the small shops in the square. I often liked to visit one of our Sunday school newlywed couples who owned and operated a small furniture company on Main Street. After visiting them, I proceeded downtown toward Dargan Street, walking by new shops where I had never been, and I noticed a window filled with kitchen paraphernalia, books, and baby gifts.

Upon entering the store, I noticed a beautiful Asian baby in a small playpen near the front window, basking in the sunshine that flowed through. An older woman sat near the baby, and a younger woman, who had to be the baby's mother because she too was strikingly beautiful, greeted me. I commented on the beauty of the small child, and both ladies smiled. I continued to shop and finally found a beautiful apron to purchase. When I opened my purse to pay for the apron, both women stood still. Neither of them came to take my money or help me.

The younger woman stepped forward and said, "No English."

I got out a bill that I knew would cover the apron and taxes and laid it on the counter. I assumed that a husband or father who could speak English had stepped out and would soon return. Both ladies smiled and accepted the bill.

As I was leaving, I laid a tract on her counter and said in a loud voice, "Please get someone to read this to you or read it after you learn English!" (She was not deaf; I spoke loudly because she couldn't speak English.) This tract says on the front, "Have a Good Day," and on the inside is a beautiful explanation of the gospel of Christ.

After I left, I felt really silly. Why would I leave a gospel tract with two women who could not speak a word of English, much less read it? As I left, I saw an Asian-looking man walk into the store. Hopefully, he could speak English. After that afternoon, I did not think of those two ladies again until ...

Three years later, I was walking down a very crowded hallway in our church. It was the change of services. We started having two services so when one group of members moved into the Sunday school department, the other group moved into the main auditorium for the second service. Hallways were packed, and sometimes we had to turn sideways to get through. During one of these midmorning swaps, a Filipino woman grabbed my arm and said in English, "It is you. I have found you!" Her accent was strong, but her words were perfect.

"Look!" she said as she pulled out a dingy and wrinkled but still legible tract I had given her. She had learned some English, enough to meet Christ, and because I had my church name on the back of that tract, she came!

Was it just by chance that I went into that store that day? Why would anyone leave an English tract where no one could speak English? Even I thought it was foolish at the time. My friend, God does not make mistakes. His Word says in Proverbs 20:24, "Man's goings are of the Lord; how can a man then understand his own way?" Trust me on this, only God!

For the Love of Cats

MY CHILDHOOD WAS NOT a happy one. We moved often when I was very young because my father was an alcoholic and had a very hard time keeping a job. Very often, we lived with one of my sisters because we no longer had a place to live. It was unsettling, but at a very young age, I learned to trust in a higher power. I would like to remember trips to Sunday school with my parents, nighttime devotions on my dad's lap, or any of the many wonderful stories I have often heard from friends and other relatives who are near my age.

My mother, who worked many jobs to support her six children, often prayed for food. Sometimes, I would hear her in the night, on her knees beside her bed, asking God to supply our needs and help us get through another week.

My mom and I were living with my sister and her husband when I remember experiencing the first answer to a direct prayer. It was very simple, and many people would believe it was just a coincidence, but in my ten-year-old mind, it had great impact. Here's my story:

My sister and her husband were barely able to support themselves, and now Mom and I were living with them. One afternoon, we were walking in her backyard and found a litter of abandoned kittens, six beautiful hungry kittens all alone and far too young to know how to hunt on their own. We searched for the mother cat but never found her. My sister informed me that she had no cat food and suggested we stop playing with the kittens and pray that God would supply food for these cuties. We did so, right in her backyard, on our knees. I will never forget that prayer. She simply asked God to take care of those kittens and supply all their needs, just like He was supplying all our needs while we were living with them. She also thanked Him for His goodness and His love for us.

Later that night, my sister's husband came home from his job at a grocery store, and you will never believe what he had in his hands. He told us a delivery truck had dropped a case of, yes, cat food. It dropped right beside his car. Several cans had been damaged, so the store owner told him to just throw away the case. He brought it home, having no idea that six baby kittens were living by the big oak tree in the backyard. There was no such thing as cell phones, and my sister had not told him of the kittens. Could it be that God had heard our prayer in the backyard and sent food to those kittens? Could it be that there was a higher power that watched out for people who were in trouble or answered prayers for little girls whose daddy never came home and whose mother was always working and sometimes crying?

These things weighed heavily on my young mind, and I had many questions. At thirteen years of age, the same sister took me to a Billy Graham crusade in Charlotte, North Carolina, and at that time, I gave my life to Jesus Christ. I had witnessed how an almighty God cared enough about kittens to send them food, simply because we asked in faith. I knew that if He loved those kittens, He loved me. This same sister instilled in me the act of giving. She taught me how to tithe before I had any idea what tithing involved.

I would like to say that I hung onto that childlike faith, but unfortunately, life got in my way. After Mom and Dad divorced, I became angry with God and decided that my life was my own. As a rebellious teenager, I agreed to marry my high school sweetheart. We were married while I was still in school, and after being married only eight months—and near graduation—I found myself pregnant. I was not prepared for a baby, but I certainly was not prepared for a husband who did not want a baby. By the time our beautiful daughter was born, he was ready for a divorce and already had another girlfriend with benefits, so I left and moved in with my other sister in South Carolina.

I know this story sounds so horrible and may bring tears to your eyes, but hold on. There is so much more to this sad story! Our God uses ordinary people, broken people, and people from all walks of life to fulfill His purposes on this earth. I really believe that going down this path in life, being in a state of rebellion, marrying the wrong person, and having a baby at such an early age has made me the person I am today. All this has caused me to seek a loving God who lets me have my own way to discover that His way is what I desire with all my heart.

My past has made me stronger in my faith. I believe it has made me a better wife to a husband who adores me (my second chance) and allowed me to be the mother of two wonderful boys and six precious girls who have grown up to be awesome adults who love the Lord and serve Him in so many different ways. Only a loving God could see all my needs and fill them before I even ask. Only God!

As for Me and My House: The Lake House

MANY YEARS AGO, MY husband and I would get in a small boat and go fishing at Lake Marion of the Santee Cooper Lakes in Manning, South Carolina. At this time, we only had two children. We would fish and travel from one bank to the other, and we often would put our boat in the water at Randolph's Landing. We would motor along the dam and back to the area where beautiful homes were, Eagle Point. It was properly named because many eagles built their nests over the waters here.

Many afternoons, we would pass beautiful homes on the banks of that lake, and many times, my husband would say, "Look at that beautiful gray house with the long dock." We looked at it every time we went fishing. It was three stories, and the entire back, facing the water, was glass. It had a garden beneath the decking full of beautiful red tomatoes and cucumbers. The pier shot out very far over the water and housed a beautiful boat in the boatshed attached to it. The grass was so green and lush that we initially thought it was Astroturf. It was manicured to perfection.

The front entrance to the house was a circle brick driveway with gardenias so fragrant that they smelled up the entire neighborhood. I could just imagine a five-tier water fountain in the middle of all that wonderful aroma.

Across the road in front of the house was another part of the lake, an inlet. Here, a beautiful archway, which I imagined was covered with jasmine, led into a sandy beach area where the boat could be parked for easy entry. This beautiful house of our dreams had water in the front and back, and best of all, my husband's very best friend and former boss owned the house next door.

Why am I telling you about this beautiful house, this house of our dreams, the house we could never afford? I am telling you because God gave us this house. He did. The man and woman, Bobby and Wanda, were good Christians. They were having some health issues and decided they needed warmer climate, so they were moving to Florida. Dan's former boss and neighbor suggested we look at the house. I wanted badly to see inside but knew we could never imagine owning such a property.

The inside of the house was as beautiful as the outside. Italian tile had been flown in from Italy and installed throughout the living quarters on the first floor. The beautiful stairway from the first floor to the second wound through the middle of the house, up to three beautiful bedrooms and baths on the top floor. The floors were a gorgeous oak with banisters to match, and all bedrooms in the entire house exposed the beautiful lake with a full view.

We told them how much we loved the house, but we left, not believing we could ever own such a beautiful place. We had such little faith back then. After several months, the couple called us and asked us to come and see the house again. They wanted to help us get the house because they had seen how much we loved it when we saw it. We explained that we could never afford it, so they reduced it by half and then, on a handshake, told us we could move in and pay them the other half after we had sold our much smaller house on the other side of the lake.

How could this be? How could we buy this beautiful house for half of its worth and get to pay the part we owed after selling our other house? On top of all that miracle, Bobby and Wanda left all the beautiful—and I mean beautiful—furniture, floral arrangements, and bed linens and comforters, and on the very day we moved into the house, she had prepared a delicious baked chicken dinner for us, which was hot in the oven when we arrived. All the beds were made and ready for sleep, and everything was in perfect order.

This reminds me of Deuteronomy 6:11 when God said He would give us houses full of all good things you did not fill (all the furniture and linens left behind), cisterns you did not dig (a well on the property), and vineyards you did not plant (gardenias, roses, and vegetables in the garden), and when you eat and are full (meal in the oven).

Of all the houses we owned during our lifetime, this will always be our favorite. It was the most beautiful, and it was a miracle from only God!

How Do I Love Thee? Let Me Count the Ways

UNTIL NOW, I HAVE shared with you almost all of the details of my life and how God has been in every little detail—the good, the bad, and the ugly. This chapter has been the hardest to write because I find it hard to share details that are so hidden. Yet, if I leave this out, then I have not told my whole story.

Because I was saved at the age of thirteen at a Billy Graham crusade in Charlotte, North Carolina, I was still saved when I was rebelling against God and doing my own thing against my mother's will, like running away to get married at seventeen. Being saved does not mean we will not go down that forbidden path. Being saved means we have asked God to forgive us of our sins, which were paid for when He sent His only Son, Jesus, to die for us. We ask Him to come into our lives and take us to be with Him when we leave this earth. I firmly believe that when we do this in sincerity and seek Him, He is with us forever, even during our worst times and our darkest hours.

When I met my first husband in school, we became high school sweethearts. I told you the story of how we feel in love, or so we thought, and how we were married while I was in my junior year of high school. I also told you that eight months later, I became pregnant in my senior year of school. Next, my first husband decided he did not want children. I gave birth to our daughter, and he left to live with another woman. I left with my daughter to live in South Carolina with my sister.

Now here is what I did not tell you. After moving in with my sister, I worked at our local A&P store in our small town of Lake City. Here, I met my husband of fifty-four years. Remember, I had left North Carolina and a husband who did not want to be either a husband or father. I was a cashier at the grocery store, and Dan was my bag boy. He had just graduated high school and planned to attend flight school in the fall. He was very handsome, and we became friends right away.

Considering all that I had been through and where I was at this time in my life, I had decided that the one thing I did not need was another man. The more I tried to stay away from this guy, the more he pursued me. Every time I took a break at work, he would take his break and follow me to the break room. He would continually ask me for a date. I explained to him that I was recently separated and not interested in dating anyone. But he continued, and I finally agreed to date him if it were a double date. We went out to eat with friends and had a wonderful time.

During this time, I was so confused. I was falling in love but had no idea what love was. After all, I thought I was in love the first time, remember? How could I know? I had almost ruined my life. I could not go down this road again.

By the end of summer, I knew he was in love with me. I was trying hard not to be in love with him, so I decided it was time for me to return to North Carolina, find a job that would support my daughter and myself, and leave this young man to go off to the Air Force Academy, where he had a scholarship. So that is exactly what I did.

He called me every day. He came to Charlotte every weekend. He refused to go on to the Air Force Academy. Finally, after I refused to return to South Carolina, he moved to Charlotte and got a job at the same bank where I worked. He was relentless.

When he asked me to marry him, I explained that I really did not know if I loved him. I told him I had thought I was in love the first time. I said, "Look at what a mess I have made!"

I will never forget what he said. He took my face into his hands, looked directly into my eyes, and said, "If you will marry me, you do not have to love me. I will love enough for both of us!"

When I decided to marry him, I rededicated my life to Christ, the same Christ who saved me at that Billy Graham crusade. The Bible says in Proverbs 28:13 that he who covers his sin will not prosper, but whoever confesses and forsakes them will have mercy. I asked God to give me a second chance at marriage. I asked Him to give me a husband who would love me and I would love in return.

He has done so much more. He has given us a love for each other that is beyond belief. We are not perfect. We make mistakes. We even ask each other for forgiveness. But we are best friends.

We love to travel together and spend our days now entertaining missionaries and pastors as well as our children and grandchildren. We love life. We love and honor the God that gave us this life, no matter how we got here. We had to travel the path we traveled in order to get here together.

This book is a testimony of God's goodness to an ordinary family who decided a long time ago that we could trust God with everything. Anything God has given us, we can trust Him with anything else we do not need! He gave this girl a second chance at marriage and children. (Remember, the doctor said I could not have another one.) He knew we wanted a big family, and the extra children He gave us have been such blessings in our lives. If we had more children naturally, we would never have had the opportunity to know and love the ones He sent to us by His hand, not by our might.

We are truly a family that has seen miracles come to life. How? Only God.

Lady, Our Wonder Dog

BEFORE EXPLAINING HOW LADY became our wonder dog, let me explain how she miraculously came into our lives. My husband and I had two—yes, two—beautiful shih tzu dogs for eighteen long years. We enjoyed these pups very much. Cookie was our girl; Oreo was our male. After both animals passed away, we decided it was time to travel, and since we both were retired, we did not want to have the problem of finding dog sitters or taking them to board for a week at a time while we were away. So both of us agreed, "No more dogs."

About six months after Oreo died at seventeen years of age, my next-door neighbor, also named Sonya—and whose husband's name was Floyd, my entire name—asked if I would mind stopping by the local animal shelter and picking up the paperwork to have her dog spayed since it was closed on her way to and from work. I gladly would do this for her on my next visit to town for groceries.

As I drove into the facility parking lot, I purposely parked where the dogs in cages and runs would not be visible to me. I did not want to see animals needing homes because my heart goes out to them, and after all, we had decided, "No more dogs for the Floyds."

I stepped out of the car and walked directly inside and got the paperwork for Sonya. On my way out of the office, I purposely kept my eyes from the long line of fencing holding many dogs, large and small.

The moment I started to open my car door, a small black-and-white, heavily matted, pitiful-looking dog weighing about fifteen pounds literally jumped right into my arms. Now this was hard to do because I was holding my phone in one hand and the paperwork for my neighbor in the other. So when this mutt jumped directly up toward my face, I immediately cupped my arms, drawing elbows together to catch her. She looked directly into my eyes, and I must admit I have never seen such sad eyes in my life, big, brown, sad eyes asking me to take her and not put her back in that cage.

Immediately, a young lady came flying around the front of my car, profusely apologizing and calling her by name, which was Amy! Who names a dog Amy? She explained she was a volunteer dog walker who came three times a week and walked the dogs for the shelter. She said she could not catch Amy. She had jumped and ran straight to me. She said this dog had been with them for about a month and she had to be moved to a high-fence dog run with a top on it because she could escape all they put her into. She said Amy would constantly jump from morning to night to the lock on the gate, hoping to hit it in some way to open it to let her out. She also told me they had found Amy tied and left under a house where the owners had left her to starve to death before moving away!

Well, I guess you know that all thoughts of not having a dog went right out the window. There was no way I could leave without that dog. So I called my sweet husband and told him what had happened and said I did not go there to pick out a dog but a dog had picked out me. When I did bring Amy, whom he renamed Lady, home, he was so glad I did. She took to us immediately, and we trained her in just a few days.

I must admit that this dog was the smartest and cheapest dog we had ever owned. She obeyed immediately. At first, she was afraid of Dan. Maybe her previous owner was rough with her, but she soon learned that he was a big snuggle bunny, and she loved him dearly. She followed me into every room and even dragged her bed into each room to watch me work. Sometimes, she would just lay in my arms and look into my eyes, saying, "Thank you so much for rescuing me." She could not write me cards or letters or call me and tell me like my girls could. She just said it all in her beautiful brown eyes.

Now you have the picture. We bathed her, cut her nails, and combed her matted hair, and she is beautiful. Because I love training dogs, she obeys all her commands in English, Spanish, and sign language.

My husband was on a trip, and I visited a friend in Charlotte, North Carolina. Of course, Lady went with me. We had her for about four months. I practiced with her daily in Shelia's backyard because she was still in training. Little did I know that Shelia's neighbor was videoing this training. She was amazed at how smart our dog was.

My second day there, we decided to do a little Christmas shopping for some decorations Shelia needed for her new home. So we locked Lady in her garage. Knowing she was an escape artist, we moved a metal storage box that weighed over a hundred pounds in front of the only hole in the garage, a small cat door for the previous owner's cat. Then we left to go shopping.

When we returned three hours later, I immediately knew something was wrong. We saw insulation on the outside of the little cat door. Running inside the house, we realized our Houdini, with her small body, had moved the metal storage box and clawed out the insulation to get to the cat door. She had escaped! We were horrified.

Shelia lived in an area of Charlotte called Bonterra, a beautiful neighborhood with probably eight hundred to one thousand homes. Yards are manicured, and kids play basketball and ride bikes all over the neighborhood. Shelia and I walked all these streets, stopped, and recruited these kids. We had literally everyone in the neighborhood looking for our precious lost dog.

After several hours, hoarse from yelling and wet from the cold and fine freezing mist that had begun to fall, we returned to Shelia's house. We both were crying, both brokenhearted and exhausted. When I returned, my husband, who is wise beyond words, called me and told me to stop crying because I was ruining my visit with my dear friend. He said if someone had stolen or picked up our dog, they would fall in love with her just like we had, and she would be in good hands. He told me God had given her to us and we had loved her well, so it was time for me to trust God and let go. I did. I got in the shower, and we settled back to watch a Hallmark movie and get our minds off what had just happened.

After several hours, the phone rang, and Shelia asked me to answer. I did, and the woman on the phone asked if I were missing a black-and-white dog. My heart jumped into my throat, and I started screaming for Shelia. She asked her name, and I told her Lady. She then called Lady, and she came to her. I was so excited. She said she was leaving for a party, and because Lady was so dirty when they found her, she had put her in the backyard with her two dogs. She assured us that she would be fine. Her brick fencing was eight feet tall. Her dogs had been there for years and never gotten out.

I calmly explained to her that I had to come and get my dog. It was freezing and sleeting outside, and she was no longer used to the cold. So she gave us her address and told us how to unlock the gate. She was leaving in fifteen minutes. I would like to tell you that we went there and got Lady and all was well, but that is not the end of this miraculous story.

We drove fifteen miles across town, only to find that Lady had climbed the eight-foot fence and escaped from her yard. We knew she could not have been gone long because we put our housecoats on over our pajamas and took off as soon as we got the call. I was so hoarse I could hardly talk, and Shelia had rolled down the windows in my little CRV. We were once again yelling her name out the window into the sleet, rain, and bitter cold. We drove through one more neighborhood, and as we were about to turn around, we saw her running as fast as she could across the street. Shelia was driving, and I was in the passenger seat. And with all my might and my hoarse voice, I called her name.

She immediately stopped, turned around, and literally jumped through the driver's seat, where Shelia was sitting, and onto my lap. Both Shelia and I were crying, but this time, they were tears of joy. She was matted, soaking wet, filthy, shivering, and full of those sticky little balls that stick in a dog's fur. But I did not mind. I held her tight, wrapped her in my housecoat, and held her all the way home. Shelia and I bathed her and combed and dried her. She had her own bed, but that night, Shelia allowed my baby to sleep in bed with me. I will always be grateful because I did not want to let go of her.

The next day, we called the woman to let her know that we had gotten Lady. We didn't let her know she had escaped her backyard. When we asked how she found our dog, it was even more miraculous! She and her daughter were shopping at Lowe's in Charlotte, ten miles from Shelia's house. This is the exact Lowe's Shelia and I had shopped hours earlier.

When she went to get in her car, Lady was there, trying to get in her car. When she opened the door, Lady jumped on her five-year-old daughter's lap. Her daughter insisted they take Lady home. She said she had no intentions of keeping her and would have taken her to the shelter the next day. But her daughter got on Facebook and found a video of Lady. (Remember the neighbor videoing me while I was training her in the backyard?) When she found out Lady was missing, she put the video on Facebook.

Do you really think all this was a coincidence? How could my dog, whom I rescued, escape from a closed-in garage, travel ten miles across Charlotte, and cross Highway 74 (a four-lane highway) to the place where we had shopped, and be picked up in a car the exact color as mine in a parking lot where we had parked just hours earlier? Not me. Only God could orchestrate such an adventure! Only God!

The Four Bears

IT WAS FOUR O'CLOCK on the morning of October 18, 2022, and there was a welcome chill in the air as I sat at our round dining table enjoying my alone time with God and His Word. We do not have an exact morning ritual because He knows how often we have guests here, and I will have often gone two or three days without meeting Him at all, but He is always here when I seek Him. He is always waiting to hear my problems, to lighten my burdens, and to bring me peace and joy no matter how chaotic my life.

After reading His Word and finishing my time in His Word, I looked out our picture window at some beautiful raccoons helping themselves to the seed in our hanging bird feeder. It was amazing to watch. The larger raccoon would reach his hand up into the feeder, grab all the seed he could get in his hand, and then hand it down to the smaller (female) raccoon, and she would eat it. They ate their fill and then left the remaining feed in the feeder.

Many of our neighbors had seen bears on their property and had sent us pictures of these massive, beautiful creatures. I had always hoped we would have one come to our property, but it had been six years, and we had never had a visitor!

As I sat in the quiet morning and just witnessed two soulmates have breakfast on our deck, I simply asked my heavenly Father to send me a bear. The prayer was simple. "Oh, God, You made them. We have been here six years. They have visited all my neighbors, and I would love to just see one. Could You please send me a bear?"

After finishing this prayer, I promptly went back to bed with my husband. When he stirred and asked what I had been doing, I told him that I had prayed and asked God to send us a bear. "Okay, honey, now get some sleep." And I did!

That very evening about seven o'clock, my husband and I were sitting on our couch in front of our fireplace watching television. Our small Havanese dog, Lady, was lying on the ottoman in front of our couch. Suddenly, I saw an enormous bear walking right in front of our picture window and just to the left of where my husband was seated. I told him not to move but to look to his left. I told him there was a big bear right outside his window. He did look, and he was surely amazed. I, on the other hand, was crying like a baby.

I remembered my prayer and knew immediately that my heavenly Father had chosen to answer it. Dan quietly turned to look at the bear, and we both tried to remain calm so as not to awaken Lady, who would have barked and scared our friend away. But to our amazement, three baby bears followed right behind the mama bear, parading all the way across our entire deck. One baby stopped and attempted to climb on our swing. They then jumped to the top of the railing, over a two hundred-foot drop, and walked the entire deck, dancing, playing, and entertaining us. Four bears, not just one.

This mama bear and her three babies stayed around our house for two full weeks. We would leave to get in our car, and Mama Bear would be standing on our waterfall right under our deck. The babies would be playing on the bottom deck. We took pictures and videos, and they would stay right out back at our firepit. Mama Bear would bed them down in leaves every night. We were astounded. Most bears go to their den at night, especially if they have babies, but ours stayed right with us. They were totally nonaggressive and seemed right at ease with us. We left about the middle of November, and we could still see them in our yard until after Thanksgiving when they left to hibernate.

We had many people tell us we were out of our minds for letting them stay so long. Some folks told us they would break into our home looking for food and do damage around our home. But we never experienced any of that. Many of our children and grandchildren would stand in our back bedroom and watch them for hours out in our backyard. When guests came, they were amazed. Missionaries from Germany spent several days here and watched them daily, and they took pictures to send to their children.

I know, beyond any shadow of a doubt, that God, my God— who parted the sea and made dry land for His people to walk on, who turned water into wine at a wedding, who healed the sick, who made the blind to see and the lame to walk, who raised the dead, who made a donkey talk and Moses' staff turn into a serpent—and I could go on and on, but you get the picture—the same God who did all that, saw fit to answer my simple prayer to see a bear. Well, I am not sure what you believe. But I know He sent these bears, and I was not afraid.

In my innocence, I asked. In His magnificence, He answered. There are only two words to describe it, only God!

The Car Miracle

WHEN THE OLDER GIRLS were married and no longer living at home, Dan and I set aside some money for a car. At this time, I was working two blocks from our home in a law office with Jack Lawson and Kevin Barth. Dan worked for Wallace Jordan at Toyota of Florence. We only had one vehicle, and Dan had to take our son to school each day. Our daughter drove a small Toyota to school and then to her work. Getting a car just for me was a big deal.

During this time, our church, Florence Baptist Temple, was having a fundraiser for a new gymnasium for our church and school. Dan and I had been tithers for many years leading up to this time in our life. We had also attended a seminar for financial planning, and for the first time in our life, we had a savings account. We had a little nest egg for that new car we were planning to buy. Also during this time, we taught a marriage class in our church, and we often would pick up couples or women with children and bring them to our church and our class.

As we sat under great teachers, we realized that God was impressing upon our hearts to give that little nest egg of $7,000 to our church instead of buying that new car. After all, my work was only two blocks away, and Dan's boss let him drive whatever he wanted to drive from his Toyota company. When he test-drove cars, he drove a different car every week. So we gave our nest egg to our building fund. I am so glad we did because we got to live another miracle.

One of Dan's dear friends worked at a computer company, Computer Land. He called us one day and asked Dan if I still needed a car. He knew Dan was looking for a car for me, but he had no idea we had given our money to the building fund. Dan explained to him that we no longer had money for a new car.

Rick Giles, who is now in heaven, said, "It's okay. You don't need money. I have a car for Sonya."

He brought us a beautiful new green Impala to our house that evening. He explained that the company had leased that car for two years and already paid the insurance for two years. The man for whom it was leased had passed away, so he brought it to us. Here we had a brand-new car, with no insurance payments, no car payments, nothing, for me for two whole years. Seven thousand dollars would not have bought that car for me.

I am so glad we listened to God and helped with the building fund. I am so glad the Holy Spirit touched our hearts and said, "Give it." But much more than that, I am so glad we got to see God work in our lives performing miracles behind the scenes, always there for us in a way that could be "only God!"

The Ten-Dollar Dress

HAVING EIGHT CHILDREN AT home was sometimes exhausting but exciting most of the time. We spent most of our time after school doing homework and preparing dinner for our large family. Because our kitchen was very small, each girl took turns learning how to prepare meals and clean up afterward. It was very organized and usually lots of fun.

One of our most precious memories happened when the girls were at school in Hemingway, South Carolina. Each of them came home very excited after school, exclaiming that the school was having a beauty contest. Four of them wanted to enter that beauty contest. There was only one problem: four girls, four dresses, four entrance fees. Having to tell them they could not enter the contest was very hard for me. These girls were beauties, inside and out! However, I knew it would be impossible for us to afford the contest.

After much deliberation, the girls came up with an idea. They would borrow dresses from their friends. Many of their friends had prom dresses, former beauty pageant dresses, and so forth. This would work. So we told them if they could borrow their dresses and come up with the entrance fee, they could enter the contest. All four of the girls entered the contest.

Each of our girls had jobs after school to make their own spending money. Our daughter Brenda worked at Cato, a clothing store in downtown Hemingway. She came home one day after school very excited because she had found a beautiful dress in the store that fit her perfectly. She had tried several of her friends' dresses, but none had fit her perfectly like this one! Of course, it fit her perfectly, but it was $300. Knowing she did not have the money to buy the dress, I reminded her that we could not help her.

The contest was just one month away, and Brenda came in after working three hours on Saturday and informed me that the dress had been put on a marked-down rack at the store. It had been marked down to $150. She asked me to please go down to the store and look at the dress with her. She tried it on for me. It was very beautiful and looked as if a talented seamstress had worked tirelessly to fit it to her beautiful body. However, she still did not have $150 saved for such an occasion.

That night, just like every other night, we all gathered on our king-sized bed to have our devotions. Brenda asked that we pray about finding her a dress for the contest. We explained to her that if it were important to her, it was important to God. We also explained that if we really believed that God heard our prayers, no matter how small, He was also capable of answering them. After all, had we not just seen Him answer Debby's prayer for clothing, and He supplied her with a beautiful coat with her name on it!

So we prayed. We prayed for each other about everything. We prayed for health because we could not afford lots of doctor and hospital bills. We prayed for provisions and always had food on the table. We prayed for contentment with ten folks living in one house with only one-and-a-half baths. And yes, we prayed and asked God to answer our precious daughter's prayer.

The dress continued to be reduced in price at Cato. It came down from $300 to $150 and then down to $50, and Brenda was ecstatic. She knew now it was in her price range, and she asked if she could purchase it on Thursday. (The contest was just two weeks away.) Of course, it was her money. It looked as if it were her dress for sure.

When Brenda went to work after school the next day, the store manager, who really liked Brenda, told her that those formal dresses would have to go. She had marked down each of them, including the one Brenda wanted, to $10 each.

The night of the pageant, our girls were so beautiful, each of them. They competed against girls who wore expensive $700 and $800 dresses. However, God made a believer of a certain young lady who had no money but lots of faith. She won Miss Hemingway High in a $10 dress.

Brenda still lives in Hemingway. She gave up a secretarial job many years ago so she could become a substitute teacher at Hemingway schools and be there with her three beautiful children and seven grandchildren as they enter school. She wants them to remember that God is there for them, just like He was and always has been there for her!

God's Word says, "Therefore I tell you, do not worry about your life, what you will eat or drink; or about your body, what you will wear. Is not life more important than food, and the body more important than clothes? Look at the birds of the air; they do not sow or reap or store away in barns, and yet your heavenly Father feeds them" (Matthew 6:25).

A young impressionable teenager and a $10 dress could only equal one thing, right? Only God!

He Sent Angels

ON MARCH 15, 2019, I was in Sarasota, Florida. My husband had left at seven in the morning to return to our home in South Carolina. At this time, he was teaching a class at our church called Radical Mentoring. He had to return home for one of those meetings. He left me there to finish decorating a small model home we had just purchased as part of our Shepherds Rest. I had several stops to make and numerous things to buy. Although I normally took Lady everywhere, I decided it was time she stay home and get familiar with the new surroundings. This was so unusual because we literally took her everywhere.

Leaving home around eleven, I went straight to the Bed Bath & Beyond, located about five miles from our house. I also stopped at Best Buy and then Kohl's. I bought dishes, comforters, pictures, fans, and artificial flowers with vases. All these things were in my trunk. It was literally loaded and packed in our 2011 CRV.

When I arrived at the entrance of our neighborhood, Sarasota Lakes RV Park, where I was decorating our model home, I was turning left, and a small orange-colored vehicle ran the red light and hit me. He did not hit me once; he hit me twice. I was talking on the phone with my daughter through the car phone. She asked what was going on, and I calmly told her I had been hit but that my car was turning upside down. As she screamed, the phone fell onto the floor, disconnecting from the car system, and I could no longer hear her.

I will never forget that feeling, his car slamming into the right side of my car, my car spinning around and his car hitting me again on my side, and then my car flying through the air and landing on the side of the road upside down. All airbags had opened. It felt as if I were flying through soft clouds and everything was in slow motion. When the car landed, I was hanging upside down in my car. The only problem was that I could not loosen the safety belt. It was stuck because I was upside down and all my weight was on it.

As only God could have it, a police officer was northbound three lanes over and saw the whole thing happen. He immediately crossed over and came to my aid.

Before he could get there, the young man who ran the stoplight came up and opened my door. "Madame, are you okay?" he asked.

I replied that I was just a little uncomfortable hanging there, so he pulled a knife from his pocket and cut my seat belt. All the windows in the entire car, except the back hatch window, were now lying on the top of the car, which at this time was the bottom. When I was finally freed from the seat belt, I landed in a pile of this glass. I crawled out of the car, and the police officer called an ambulance when he saw the very little blood on my shoulder.

I crawled from the car and stood with the officer and the young man who hit me. He was late for work and in a big hurry. He thought he could get through the red light before another car, my car, came. He was not hurt but went to the hospital in the ambulance to be checked out.

After arguing with the police officer, I waited for another officer. (In Florida, it had to be two of them.) One waits for the car to be towed; the other waits with the victim to make sure they either get home or to the hospital.

My car was at the entrance of where I lived. I told the police officer that my dog was at home and I needed to get there. My precious neighbors came to the rescue in their golf cart and took me home. (Thank you, Donna Case.) There was no scratch on my body except the little one on my shoulder from the glass. Now this is where the story gets really interesting.

The police officer called my husband and told him that I had refused to go to the hospital. Of course, my husband called the neighbors who had rescued me and asked them to please take me to be checked out. He told me if I did not go right away, he would hop on a plane and come to Sarasota. I knew he would do it, and then he would miss his meeting with Radical Mentoring. So I agreed to go.

When we arrived at the hospital, there were twenty-six people in the waiting room of the ER. My dear friends were in the car waiting for me. How could I keep them there for five or six hours or all night? I prayed and asked God to help me. "Please, Father, I am number twenty-seven, and I cannot be here all night." The older couple who brought me to the hospital were outside waiting in their car because they were afraid they might get sick from the ER occupants. This was a possibility for sure.

I sat down in the last available chair. A beautiful Hispanic woman with raven-black hair down to her waist sat down beside me. She seemed distraught, and I could tell she had been crying. Having a little Spanish under my belt, I started to comfort her and tell her that I would be glad to pray with her. I always take tracts, both English and Spanish, with me that clearly tell the gospel of Jesus Christ. I got a Spanish one out and handed it to her. I went over it with her, and she smiled and said she understood and would do what the tract said, which was to give her life to Christ. We both cried and hugged, and then I was called back to see the doctors.

The young man who came to get me announced that he was taking me to the fast tract because they had pictures of my car, which was still on the highway, and were sure I needed immediate attention. Two doctors and two nurses checked every inch of my body for bruises or injuries. None were found. Next, I had an MRI, and nothing was found there either. The doctor gave me some pain tablets and told me that it would be impossible for me not to be sore in the next few days and that I should be prepared.

When I got home that night and went to bed, I assumed I would not be able to move very well the next morning. As a matter of fact, when I awoke the next morning, I lay very still for a few moments and then slowly got out of bed. To my astonishment, I had no soreness, not one muscle. Also, it occurred to me that my hip, which had previously caused me much pain and suffering—and had been x-rayed and examined by five different chiropractors and medical doctors—was no longer hurting me. It usually pained me greatly to get out of bed and would start hurting again if I went up steps or stressed it in any way. But now, there was no pain. It took me several weeks to realize that during my accident and being thrown upside down in that car, my hip was completely healed. And I didn't ever take one of those pain pills.

I have no doubt that God sent angels to carry my car to safety on the side of that road. Every person entering our community in our Sarasota RV resort saw my car for six hours on the side of the six-lane highway before it was towed away. This was on Friday at 2:00 p.m. When I walked into our church unharmed on Sunday morning, I was received with joy, clapping, and rejoicing. I gave my testimony that day. What a wonderful God we serve. Only God knows why these events happened in my life. He kept me safe from all harm. Only God can send you angels exactly when you need them.

Many people who read this book may think that all of the above was just coincidental. Really? The people who saw my car upside down with all windows broken and sides crushed lying on the side of the six-lane highway at the entrance of our neighborhood saw me come into our church service two days later on Sunday without a scratch on my body. The police officer who stayed with me was a Christian. He said he had definitely seen a miracle when he saw me crawl out of that car and when he checked on me later that night and found I had been discharged from the hospital with a clean bill of health. Of course there was the ER waiting room full of people, and God sat me right beside someone who needed Jesus in her life. I was in and out of the hospital in less than one hour, back home in my bed with my dog, safe and sound.

Psalm 91:11 says, "For He will order his angels to protect you wherever you go. They will hold you up with their hands so you won't even hurt your foot on a stone." Who did this for me? Only God!

The End Is Just the Beginning

I HOPE BY NOW you have read enough about our lives to know that this book is about giving honor and glory to the only one worthy of honor and glory, only God. He has been with this family for generations, and we look forward to seeing what He has planned for us in the future here on earth and in our heavenly future with Him.

The miracles He has performed in our lives have been witnessed by not only our family but by our friends and relatives alike. He has taken us through trials and opened doors when we were totally at a loss as to where to go or what to do next. He has opened the windows of heaven and showered us with blessings we never expected, and we still stand in awe of His goodness and mercy.

If you are reading this book and have not yet experienced the miracle of His saving grace, please consider what He has done for you. He sent His only Son, Jesus, and if you had been the only person on this earth, He would still have sent Him. Why? Because He loves you! He loves you when you are angry, rebel, refuse to do right, are straight or gay, or are addicted. No sin on earth can keep you from the love of God. The only thing that can keep you from Him is you.

In my life, He is the God of the second chance (and many more), and He has proven time and time again that He can take care of my family and me, even in times when we are not where we should be in life. He's still there for us. It is His nature to be the God of many chances. Pick up His Word. Find out who He is and allow Him to become your only God!

Printed in the USA
CPSIA information can be obtained
at www.ICGtesting.com
CBHW021209150824
13133CB00012B/353